Making
Miniature Oriental
Rugs & Carpets

The Annunciation, with Saint Emidius
Carlo Crivelli

Making Miniature Oriental Rugs & Carpets

Meik and Ian McNaughton

GUILD OF MASTER CRAFTSMAN PUBLICATIONS LTD

First published 1998 by
Guild of Master Craftsman Publications Ltd,
166 High Street, Lewes, East Sussex BN7 1XU

© Meik and Ian McNaughton 1998

ISBN 1 86108 066 2

The publishers would like to thank the Trustees of the National Gallery,
London, for their kind permission to reproduce *The Annunciation, with
Saint Emidius*, on page *ii*

Photography by Peter Wright
Colour charts computer-generated by Peter Rhodes
Line drawings by John Yates

Designed by Teresa Dearlove
Typefaces: Cygnet and Cheltenham
Colour origination by Viscan Graphics P.L.
Printed and bound by Kyodo Printing Singapore
under the supervision of MRM Graphics,
Winslow, Buckinghamshire, UK.

Measurements

Although care has been taken to ensure that imperial measurements are true and accurate, they are only conversions from metric. Throughout the book instances may be found where a metric measurement has slightly varying imperial equivalents, because in each particular case the closest imperial equivalent has been given. Care should be taken to use either imperial or metric measurements consistently.

Contents

The Caucasus

Iran

Central Asia

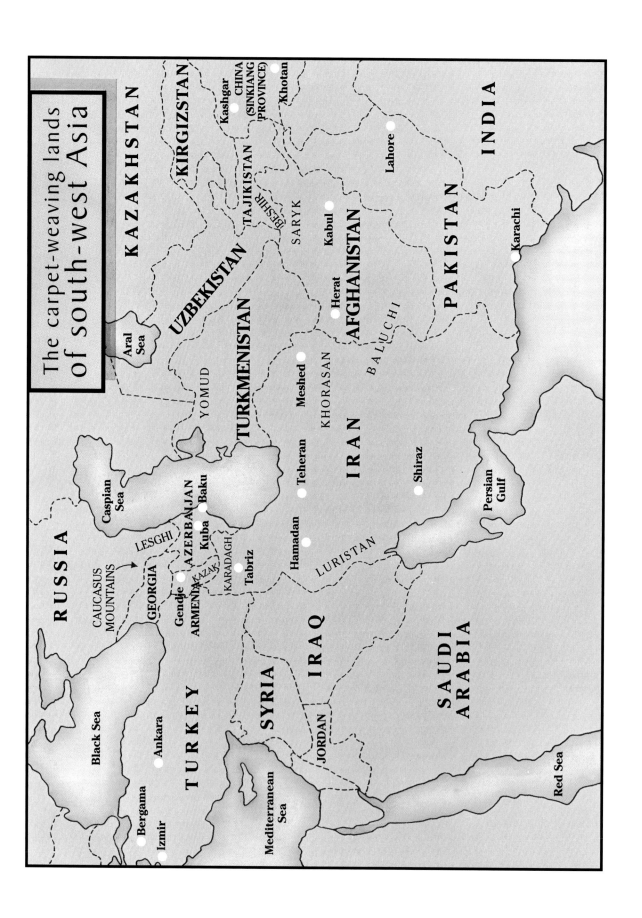

The carpet-weaving lands
of south-west Asia

RUSSIA

Black Sea

Ankara

TURKEY

Bergama

Izmir

Mediterranean
Sea

SYRIA

JORDAN

IRAQ

SAUDI
ARABIA

Red Sea

Caspian
Sea

CAUCASUS
MOUNTAINS

GEORGIA

LESGHI

AZERBAIJAN

Kuba

Baku

Gendje

KAZAK

ARMENIA

KARADAGH

Tabriz

Hamadan

Teheran

LURISTAN

Meshed

KHORASAN

IRAN

Shiraz

Persian
Gulf

Aral
Sea

UZBEKISTAN

YOMUD

TURKMENISTAN

BESHIR

SARYK

Herat

Kabul

AFGHANISTAN

BALUCHI

KAZAKHSTAN

KIRGIZSTAN

TAJIKISTAN

Kashgar

CHINA
(SINKIANG
PROVINCE)

Khotan

Lahore

PAKISTAN

Karachi

INDIA

Introduction

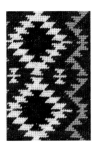MY WIFE and I have been interested in oriental rugs and carpets for many years. In fact, the very first rug I acquired was a small Baluchi prayer rug bought in Damascus in 1950. It was similar to the one shown on page 71, with hands portrayed on either side of the *mihrab* (the niche in a mosque which indicates the direction of Mecca). Since then we have steadily increased our collection. Most of the carpets we own are tribal rugs or products of cottage industries rather than large carpets made in workshops or factories.

When our granddaughter, a dolls' house enthusiast, asked my wife, who is an experienced needleworker, to make her a miniature rug, of course it had to be an oriental one. A search for a suitable pattern in various publications met with no success: such patterns as there were seemed to us just crude caricatures of the oriental styles and, in every case, the chart provided was in black and white at a very small scale and extremely difficult to follow.

We decided that, between us, we could do better. To start with, I looked at the problem from a dimensional stand-point. A carpet for a dolls' house in the conventional 1/12 scale need not be larger than about 200 x 125mm (8 x 5in) and in many cases 150 x 100mm (6 x 4in) would be big enough. With this scale in mind we needed to look only at rugs under 2.5m (8ft) in length and choose designs which could be miniaturized without losing the essential features and character of the original.

Even when narrowing the field of choice to this extent, there was still the problem of fitting the maximum amount of realistic detail into a small area. This meant using the highest stitch count with which it was practical to work. My wife made one trial carpet on 26-count material using DMC stranded cotton. This was successful but proved too fine for working with crewel wool, which she preferred to use. The rest of our miniature rugs and carpets have all been worked on 24-count canvas with crewel wool.

The next important step was to produce a charted pattern that was clear and easy to follow. This meant that it had to be in colour and at a larger scale than the finished carpet. Our original charts were made on graph paper ruled in inches and tenths and the more heavily ruled inch lines were invaluable guides when following the pattern. We did not match the colours for the chart too closely to those of the real threads, but concentrated on contrast and clarity instead.

Increasingly fascinated by the task of scaling down full-size oriental carpet designs to suit dolls' house proportions, we searched out suitable subjects for adaptation. Looking through reference books and monographs on oriental carpets we chose examples with attractive features, which were typical of the region of origin and free from too much fussy detail. Reluctantly, we had to pass over carpets from the famous weaving centres of Iran such as Isfahan, Kashan and Tabriz. Their beautiful and complex floral designs could never survive the process of miniaturization.

'Rome was not built in a day', as the saying goes, and it took a long time to develop each design and longer still to stitch each carpet. We pressed on nonetheless, aiming to complete 25 designs for this book, with a wide geographical spread covering all the principal weaving areas. Six of the designs are based on rugs from our own collection. One is based on the Carlo Crivelli painting shown as the frontispiece (see design 1, page 14). The other eighteen are based on photographs found in various publications, and a list of the books we used as sources can be found on page 102.

For the purposes of this book, the designs are grouped in four sections, covering Turkey, the Caucasus, Iran and Central Asia, the latter to include Afghanistan and Turkestan. We have tried to include both antique and more modern examples in each section, to widen the choice on offer. In this way, the similarities in design within each region can be appreciated and the contrasts between one region and another underlined.

The origin of all oriental carpet weaving lies in Central Asia among the nomadic Turkic-speaking peoples of more than two millennia ago. The westward movement of these tribes across the steppes of Russia and through Persia into the Caucasus and Asian Turkey (Anatolia), reaching the shores of the Aegean Sea around the eleventh century (AD), spread their weaving skills through all the areas covered in this book. It is interesting to compare the first and last designs included. The first (see page 14) is based on a carpet woven in Anatolia in the fifteenth century, while the last (see page 93) is based on a carpet woven in Chinese Turkestan in the twentieth century, but both have almost identical main border patterns derived from the decorative Islamic Kufic script.

This book is primarily intended to provide dolls' house enthusiasts with a range of rug and carpet designs to suit most furnishing schemes. We hope it will also appeal to those who do needlework for its own sake and who may find added satisfaction in stitching 1/12 scale versions of genuine oriental carpets. Each design is presented with a picture of the finished piece, a little information about its background, and a clear colour chart from which to work.

We would suggest that some previous needlework experience is helpful, as the designs are intricate (for the less confident, the Kuba rug on page 40 would be a good place to start, as the design is straightforward). Advice on materials and techniques is given in the next chapter, together with some points to consider should you wish to go on to design your own carpets.

Ian McNaughton

Materials and Techniques

Materials

Canvas

ALL THE carpets in this book should be worked on 24-count canvas. Included in the information for each design is a precise stitch count and an approximate finished size for the piece. When cutting the canvas for a particular carpet, allow about 75mm (3in) extra at each end and 50mm (2in) on each side. This will make it much easier to block or stretch the finished work.

With a very fine-pointed pencil (never a biro as it can show through the paler threads) mark the central lines on the canvas (indicated by small arrows on each chart) and then the heavier lines shown on the chart. These should come every 10 holes and will serve as helpful guidelines when counting stitches and following the pattern. Using such guidelines will also mean that you can spot mistakes at an early stage, so unpicking should not be so depressing as it might otherwise be. It is important, therefore, to check carefully that the marking out is correct before proceeding further.

Frames

There are several types of small frame available, but the choice of which to use is a very personal thing. It is, of course, possible to work without a frame if you prefer, but this does make straightening the finished work much more difficult. If you are using a frame to keep the canvas taut, you will find it necessary to make each individual stitch in two separate movements, with a hand on either side of the frame. This may seem cumbersome to begin with, but it quickly becomes much easier.

Threads

The thread recommended for working these rugs is Appletons crewel wool. A single strand will suffice. This wool is very fine and soft, so do not use threads longer than 30–35cm (12–14in) as they tend to pull apart with wear. If the wool looks very thin at any point, it is best to cut that part out before starting to stitch, but sometimes the thin parts only appear after work has begun. When this happens, the easiest thing is to work two stitches on top of one another.

Alternatively, two threads of stranded cotton (Anchor or DMC) can be used. Stranded cotton is easier to work with than crewel wool, but does not give such a warm and realistic finish. It is also harder to block and stretch than wool.

The suggested shade numbers given for each rug apply to Appletons crewel wool, but a table of equivalent shade numbers for Anchor and DMC cottons can be found on page 96. (The colours used on the charts have been chosen for clarity and contrast rather than accurate matching to the colours of the rugs themselves.)

Needles

Use a size 24 tapestry needle with a single strand of Appletons crewel wool, or a size 26 needle with two threads of Anchor or DMC stranded cotton. As with frames, however, the size of needle is really a matter of personal choice: some people like working with small needles, others do not.

Techniques

Tent stitch

All the carpets are worked in tent stitch (see diagrams below) which gives the neatest and flattest finish. Try to keep the back of the carpet as tidy as possible and looking almost the same as the front by working the casting-on and -off thread ends underneath the stitching on the back. If the back is kept neat, there should be no need for any backing fabric to be used.

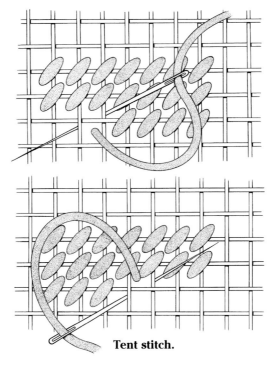

Tent stitch.

Where to start stitching

The best place to start stitching seems to be a matter for debate. Some recommend beginning in the middle of the design, but it seems more logical to start on the centre line at one end of the carpet. Make sure that you have got the position of this central line exactly right as indicated on the chart, then work the border first, using just one colour for a

Materials and Techniques

while. Everyone has their own preferred method of working, however, and it is difficult to lay down any hard and fast rules.

Mistakes

If you make a mistake and discover your error before you have worked too many more stitches, simply unpick back to the incorrect part and put it right. As long as you check back frequently against the chart and the gridlines marked on the canvas, a mistake should never be too serious. Once the work is finished, if you discover that one stitch is in the wrong colour, it is often possible to cover this with a stitch of the right colour. If a small mistake on your oriental rug cannot be rectified, just remember the old saying, 'Only Allah is perfect'.

Blocking

When the stitching is finished, remove the canvas from the frame and block it to straighten the carpet. Dampen the canvas and stretch it out on a board with drawing pins, taking care to ensure that the corners are square and the sides parallel. Leave it on the board until the threads are quite dry.

Finishing the long side edges

To finish off the long side edges of the carpet, cut the excess canvas back to two threads and then work a plaited edging stitch into the last row of stitching, following the steps given below and starting at the top right-hand corner with the cut edge of the canvas uppermost (see also diagrams opposite).

1　Bring the needle from the back of the canvas to the front, leaving 50mm (2in) of wool lying along the top edge (where it can be held by your free hand). This will be covered by subsequent stitches.
2　Take the needle through the next hole to the left, again from back to front.

3 Now take the needle back to the original hole again, thus forming an 'x' stitch over the top of the canvas.
4 Carry the needle forward three holes (i.e. missing out two holes) and bring it through the canvas from back to front.
5 Then take the needle back two holes (i.e. missing out one) and bring it through the canvas from back to front once more.

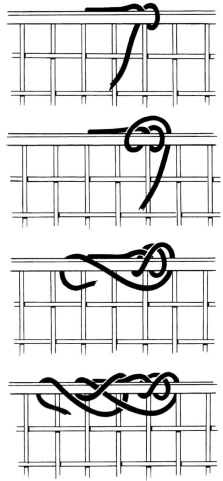

Plaited edging stitch for the long sides.

Continue the plait, taking the needle three holes on and two holes back as set out above, always remembering that the needle should pass through the canvas from back to front.

Materials and
Techniques

Fringing the ends

The fringes at either end of the rug should be worked in a Turkey or Ghiordes knot. Using a double thread, take this through the canvas as shown in the diagram below and pull the knot fairly tight. The knots should be worked through the row of holes immediately after the last row of stitching. Leave a loop of about 20mm (¾in) before moving on to the next hole. The wool can be passed round a pencil to form even loops, but the end of a finger is just as good and much simpler.

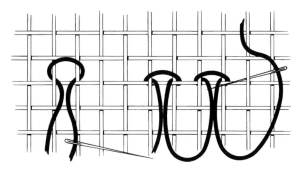

**Turkey or Ghiordes knot for the fringes
on the short ends of the rug.**

When the knotting is complete, cut the loops and trim the ends to form a neat fringe. Finally trim the excess canvas back to three threads and use a little Copydex or other adhesive to fix the underside of the fringe to it.

Designing your own carpets

After studying this book and following the charts to stitch some of the carpets featured here, you may feel that you would like to make a miniature version of your own favourite fireside rug. The following points will help you to produce a workable design.

1 The rug you select for miniaturization should have a recti-

linear pattern, free from curved lines, and the general layout should be bold without fussy detail. This will mean that the design can be adapted to the smaller scale without too much character being lost.

2 Establish the approximate size of the proposed miniature at 1/12 scale and with 24 stitches to the inch (to match the 24-count canvas). If, for example, your original rug measures 183 x 122cm (6 x 4ft), the 1/12 scale miniature at 15 x 10cm (6 x 4in) will be about 144 x 96 stitches. The exact size will emerge later.

3 Look at the proportions of your rug and, in particular, the relative widths of the field and borders. Commonly the field width is about three-fifths of the total width. In the example mentioned above, therefore, the field would be about 57 stitches wide, with each border 19 stitches wide, but you will need to work out the proportions to suit your own rug.

4 Study the main border of your rug and sketch its principal repeating motif, reducing the size of the design as far as possible without losing the basic idea behind it. Work out how many times this repeat will fit into the available length and width of the miniature, allowing for the narrow subsidiary borders or 'guards'.

5 With the borders fixed, you can establish the final overall size of the rug and the size of the field will also become clear in the process. Remember that normally the field must have an odd number of stitches in both length and width because of the centre lines. You may also need to make small adjustments to the length and width to ensure that the corner patterns fit neatly (often the hardest part).

6 Draw out the field on squared paper and mark the centre lines. Fit the main field motifs into the space available by reducing their sizes in proportion to the miniature. In the case of small repeated motifs, the total number can be reduced in order to improve clarity.

7 Draw out the complete chart for the rug, including borders, and colour in the squares appropriately.

TURKEY

RUSSIA

CAUCASUS
MOUNTAINS

Black Sea

GEORGIA

LESGHI

Bergama

Izmir

Ankara

Gendje

TURKEY

ARMENIA

KAZAK

KARADAGH

Tabriz

Mediterranean
Sea

SYRIA

JORDAN

IRAQ

Hamadan

Introduction

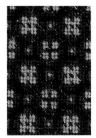ORIENTAL carpets have been coming to Western Europe for over five hundred years. During the fifteenth and sixteenth centuries they were rare and expensive status symbols of which only a few have survived to the present day. However, a number appear in paintings of the period in sufficient detail to enable their origin to be established. Most were woven in Asian Turkey (Anatolia) in villages close to the Aegean seaboard and they were probably shipped from Smyrna (Izmir) to Venice, then an important trading centre. The first two designs in this book (see pages 14 and 17) are based on carpets of this kind and are recommended for those who want a really antique look on their dolls' house floor.

The basic design of many Turkish weavings is that of a prayer rug with an arch or *mihrab* at one end, sometimes with a stylized representation of a mosque lamp hanging in it. During the seventeenth century many small rugs rather like double-ended prayer rugs were exported to Europe. Many survive in Protestant churches in Transylvania, now part of Romania. They are commonly referred to as 'Transylvanian' carpets and an example is included on page 20.

Carpet weaving continues in Turkey to the present day, with official encouragement, as a cottage industry in villages with a centuries-old tradition. Natural vegetable dyes have even been reintroduced for use on the yarns.

In central and eastern Turkey, nomadic tribes produce flat-woven kelims in bold patterns and bright colours. The example on page 23 is in the form of a double-ended prayer rug.

13

1

Large-patterned 'Holbein' Carpet

FIFTEENTH CENTURY

Size (excluding fringes): 171 x 110mm (6¾ x 4¼in)
Stitch count: 157 x 101

DURING the fifteenth century carpets from Turkish weaving centres in Asia Minor started to reach Western Europe in commercial quantities. Very few have survived, but quite a number appear in paintings and tapestries of the period. This design is based on a carpet in a painting by Carlo Crivelli, dated 1486 (reproduced on page *ii*). The carpet can be seen in the picture hanging out of an upstairs window. Carpets of this kind, with two or three large octagons filling the field, have become known as 'Holbein' carpets, although this is something of a misnomer since they first appeared long before Hans Holbein began to paint. This particular pattern is believed to have originated in Bergama.

	149		504
	748		404
	843		992

15

TURKEY
Large-patterned
'Holbein' Carpet

2

Small-patterned 'Holbein' Carpet

FIFTEENTH CENTURY

Size (excluding fringes): 177 x 101mm (7 x 4in)
Stitch count: 157 x 97

THIS PATTERN is of the same period as the first carpet and the original was probably also woven in Bergama. This time the whole field and main border are filled with repeated small octagons. A carpet with this pattern appears in a French Gobelin tapestry, one of a series entitled 'The Lady and the Unicorn' woven in Tours in about 1510.

■	209	■	914
■	926	■	332
■	935	□	988

Miniature
Oriental Rugs
and Carpets

3

Anatolian 'Transylvanian' Carpet

c.1700

Size (excluding fringes): 141 x 110mm (5½ x 4¼in)
Stitch count: 131 x 101

THIS DESIGN is based on a late-seventeenth-century example of what is known as a 'Transylvanian' carpet (see page 13). The wide main border is characteristic of the style, filled with cartouches in contrasting colours. The field has the typical form of a double-ended prayer rug, but with a vase of flowers at each end instead of a mosque lamp. With its bright colours, the whole effect is very decorative.

■	503		□	992
■	749		■	742
■	546		■	843

21

TURKEY
Anatolian
'Transylvanian'
Carpet

4

Modern Turkish Kelim

TWENTIETH CENTURY

Size (excluding fringes): 145 x 104mm (5¾ x 4⅛in)
Stitch count: 131 x 99

THERE ARE still a number of nomadic or semi-nomadic groups living in the mountainous areas of central and eastern Anatolia, who weave pileless, smooth-surfaced carpets known as kelims. Their patterns are bold and colourful and they are woven in a variety of sizes for all kinds of domestic use. This example has a traditional 'palm leaf' border, with the field in the form of a double-ended prayer rug.

■	866	□	842
■	824	□	992
■	462		

Miniature
Oriental Rugs
and Carpets

THE CAUCASUS

RUSSIA

Black
Sea

CAUCASUS
MOUNTAINS

Caspian
Sea

GEORGIA

LESGHI

Gendje

AZERBAIJAN

ARMENIA

KAZAK

Kuba

Baku

TURKEY

KARADAGH

Tabriz

SYRIA

Hamadan

Teheran

IRAQ

IRAN

Introduction

 THE CAUCASUS Mountains, stretching from the Black Sea to the Caspian Sea, and the surrounding area are home to a number of distinct ethnic groups with their own languages, religions and characters. Carpet weaving has been carried out in the region for many centuries and, although each weaving area has its own distinctive patterns, common characteristics include the use of bold primary colours and straight lines rather than curves to outline the various features of the pattern. Caucasian rugs are generally fairly small, seldom exceeding 2m (just over 2yds) in length, and this makes them very suitable for miniaturization.

The best of Caucasian weaving dates from the nineteenth century, at the start of which the area was under Persian domination. Most of our featured carpets have designs dating from that time. Many of the designs and motifs used are derived from earlier Persian weaving, although they have become distorted as time has passed. During the twentieth century, under Soviet influence, much of the weaving was concentrated in workshops and collectives and the earlier free designs became stilted and less attractive.

Amongst the principal weaving areas was Kazak in the southern Caucasus, in the state of Azerbaijan. Bright colours and bold patterns make Kazak rugs easy to recognize (see pages 28 and 31). In nearby Armenia the weaving centre of Gendje was noted for carpets that were long in relation to their width, with the field filled with diagonal bands of various colours, usually decorated with equally spaced small motifs (see pages 34 and 37).

On the eastern slopes of the Caucasus, close to the shore of the Caspian Sea, several weaving centres produced carpets with a series of cruciform stars or banners down the centre of the field, surrounded by a variety of small motifs. Three examples are included here, from Kuba, Karagashli and the Lesghi area (see pages 40, 43 and 46).

5

Kazak Rug

c. 1800

Size (excluding fringes): 145 x 106mm (5¾ x 4⅛in)

Stitch count: 129 x 101

A VARIETY of bold designs characterize the weavings of the Kazak area, but the consistent use of strong primary colours always gives a clue to the carpet's origin. This example, based on a rug dating from the very early nineteenth century, has its field filled with cruciform stars in a range of contrasting colours, which is indicative of its Kazak origin.

■	504	■	186
■	852	■	925
■	696	■	843
■	404	□	989

THE
CAUCASUS
Kazak Rug

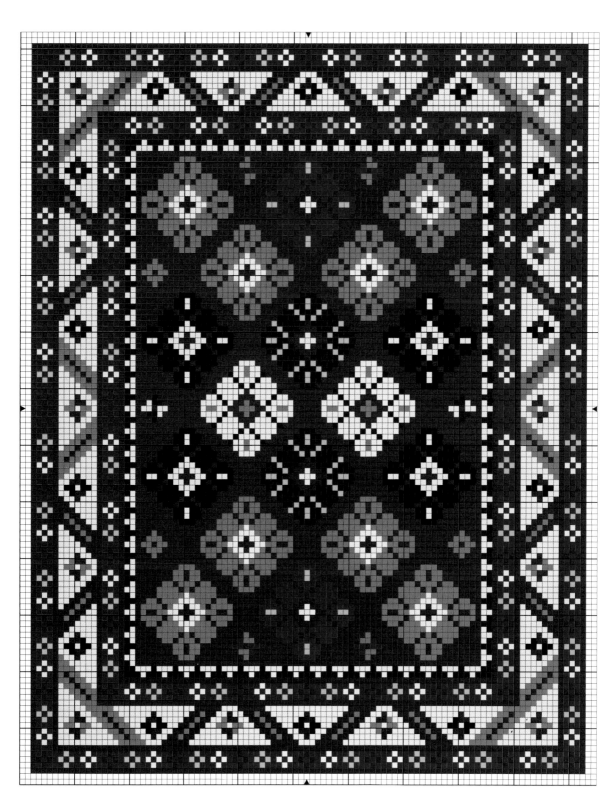

6

Kazak Rug

NINETEENTH CENTURY

Size (excluding fringes): 160 x 105mm (6¼ x 4⅛in)

Stitch count: 145 x 101

ONE GLANCE at this rug should be enough to identify it as a Kazak; its powerful design and strong colours leave no room for doubt. All the same, its design is unusual, featuring a field within a field within a field. It would go well with many modern furnishing schemes.

■	504		311
■	748		989
■	295		185

Miniature
Oriental Rugs
and Carpets

7

Gendje Runner

LATE-NINETEENTH CENTURY

Size (excluding fringes): 200 x 93mm (8 x 3¾in)

Stitch count: 183 x 87

GENDJE is in the southern Caucasus, midway between the Black Sea and the Caspian Sea. It has long been an important trading post for carpets, many of which are woven by Armenians. A typical design has the field filled with a series of diagonal bands in a repeating range of colours, each band containing repeated small motifs, in this case the comma-like *botehs*. Gendje carpets are often long in relation to their width, and these are usually described as 'runners'.

■	505	▨	742
■	503	▫	842
■	749	▫	992

**THE
CAUCASUS**
Gendje Runner

8

Armenian Gendje Carpet

MID-NINETEENTH CENTURY

Size (excluding fringes): 202 x 109mm (8 x 4¼in)

Stitch count: 181 x 101

THE CARPET on which this design is based is dedicated in Armenian script and dated 1859, and was probably woven for an Armenian church. The field is filled with a repeated pattern of crosses, stressing its Christian origin, subtly arranged to display the diagonal bands of different colours typical of Gendje weaving.

The original carpet in this case was rather too long at nearly 3m (10ft) to be scaled down accurately for the average dolls' house. In preparing the design we therefore shortened the field somewhat, to achieve the finished size given above. If you wish to work the carpet in its original proportions, the field must be lengthened by 40 stitches (at either end). In this way the border pattern can be retained without alteration as it also has a 40-stitch repeat.

■	504	■	755
■	748	■	742
■	358	■	334
■	473	□	988

THE CAUCASUS
Armenian Gendje Carpet

Miniature
Oriental Rugs
and Carpets

9

Kuba Rug

c. 1800

Size (excluding fringes): 150 x 96mm (6 x 3¾in)

Stitch count: 139 x 87

KUBA LIES near the western shore of the Caspian Sea in the north of Azerbaijan. This rug is of early design, with a severely geometric pattern. The S-border and colouring are characteristic. For those who have not previously worked on 24-count canvas, this would be a good project to start off with, since the pattern is relatively straightforward.

■	504		▤	922
□	842		▢	992
▨	926			

41

**THE
CAUCASUS**
Kuba Rug

10

Karagashli Rug

MID-NINETEENTH CENTURY

Size (excluding fringes): 177 x 102mm (7 x 4in)

Stitch count: 159 x 99

KARAGASHLI is a village near Kuba in the eastern Caucasus. Many carpets woven there display a series of banner-like red rhomboids on a turquoise background, surrounded by white cruciform stars and strange, bird-like motifs. The pattern in the main border is known as a 'leaf and chalice' pattern. It is not peculiar to Karagashli, but is widely used in Caucasian weaving.

505	692
644	989
641	928

11

Lesghi Rug

NINETEENTH CENTURY

Size (excluding fringes): 173 x 103mm (6¾ x 4in)

Stitch count: 157 x 97

THE LESGHI are a former nomadic people now settled in the north-east of the Caucasus. The elaborate geometric stars with alternate colour reversal are characteristic of Lesghi weaving. The border of this rug shows, once again, a version of the 'leaf and chalice' pattern.

■	505	■	503
■	747	▨	922
■	547	▨	544
□	842	▨	992

THE
CAUCASUS
Lesghi Rug

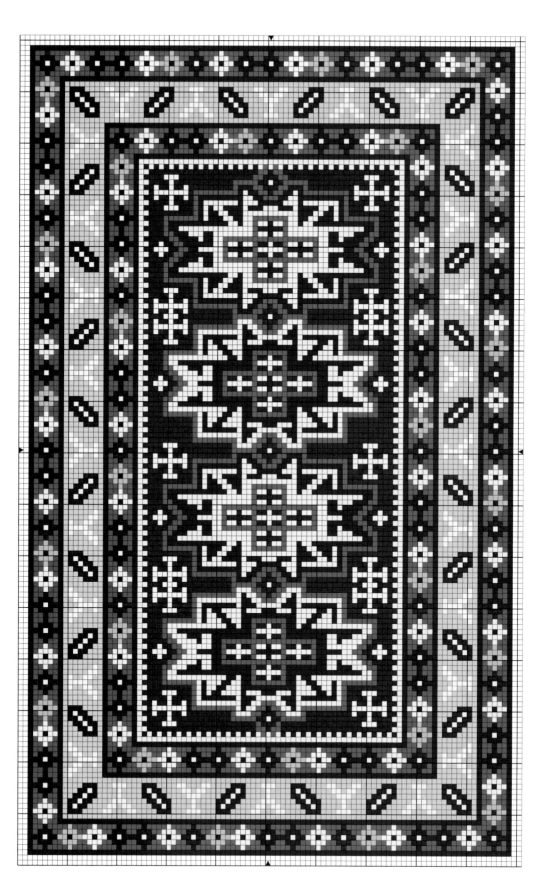

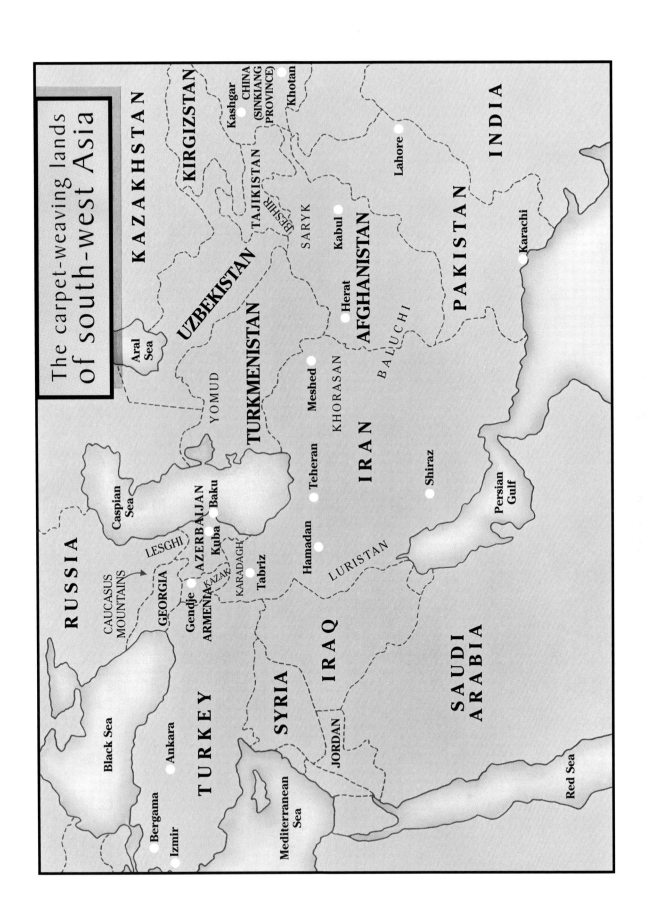

The carpet-weaving lands
of south-west Asia

KAZAKHSTAN

KIRGIZSTAN

CHINA
(SINKIANG
PROVINCE)

Kashgar

Khotan

TAJIKISTAN

INDIA

BESHIR

SARYK

Lahore

UZBEKISTAN

Kabul

PAKISTAN

TURKMENISTAN

AFGHANISTAN

Herat

Karachi

Aral
Sea

BALUCHI

YOMUD

Meshed

KHORASAN

Caspian
Sea

Teheran

IRAN

Baku

AZERBAIJAN

Shiraz

LESGHI

Kuba

Hamadan

Persian
Gulf

RUSSIA

CAUCASUS
MOUNTAINS

Tabriz

KAZAK

KARADAGH

LURISTAN

GEORGIA

Gendje

ARMENIA

Black Sea

TURKEY

SYRIA

IRAQ

SAUDI
ARABIA

Ankara

Bergama

JORDAN

Izmir

Mediterranean
Sea

Red Sea

IRAN

Introduction

AS EXPLAINED earlier (see page 2), our book does not include any examples from the famous carpet workshops of central Iran. Nevertheless, there are a number of provincial centres and tribal areas which produce material very suitable for miniaturization.

In the extreme north-west of Iran, close to the frontiers with Armenia and Azerbaijan, it is not surprising to find carpets displaying features similar to those found in Caucasian weaving, with straight lines rather than curves dominating the field. One example, from Karadagh, is included in this section (see page 52).

Further to the south lies the city of Hamadan, centre of a large weaving area. Many Hamadan carpets are woven on a cotton base and thus the fringes are often in plaited cotton. We have included one example from this area (see page 55), a design known as a Mazlaghan.

To the south-west of Hamadan, in the mountains along the border with Iraq, there are several nomadic tribes, including the Lurs, who produce rugs with primitive patterns in bright, strong colours, such as the design shown on page 58.

Even further south, not far from the Persian Gulf, is the town of Shiraz, the capital of the hilly Fars region. It is the trading centre for carpets made by several nomadic tribes in the area, whose soft, all-wool weavings are marketed as Shiraz. An early-twentieth-century example is featured on page 61.

At the eastern end of Iran, along the border with Afghanistan, live various Baluchi tribes, some settled in villages and some still nomadic. They produce a variety of rugs and carpets in a characteristic range of colours, including reds, browns and dark blue, with a field background often in a natural camel hair shade. Their patterns and motifs have been influenced by both Persian and Turkoman weavings, and four examples from this area are included here (pages 64, 67, 70 and 73).

12

Karadagh Rug

c. 1900

Size (excluding fringes): 154 x 108mm (6⅛ x 4¼in)

Stitch count: 141 x 103

CARPETS from north-west Iran, bordering on Azerbaijan, often have geometric features similar to those of the adjacent Caucasian weaving areas. They can also incorporate human and animal figures. The borders in this example from Karadagh show clear Persian influences, including the use of *botehs* (see page 73) and meandering lines, although the latter are in straight sections rather than curves. The original of this design has been in Meik's family for many years.

■	207	▨	321
▨	203	▨	186
■	852	□	691

53

IRAN
Karadagh Rug

13

Mazlaghan Rug

TWENTIETH CENTURY

Size (excluding fringes): 173 x 108mm (6¾ x 4¼in)

Stitch count: 159 x 103

RUGS WITH this lightning-like line enclosing the inner field come from the village of Kerdar, near Hamadan, in western Iran. The outer corners of the field are always closely filled with strings of rosettes and stars on a dark blue background. The triple border is typical of the Hamadan weaving area. The original of this design is woven on a cotton base, with plaited cotton fringes.

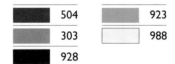

■	504	▨	923
▨	303	□	988
■	928		

IRAN
Mazlaghan Rug

Miniature
Oriental Rugs
and Carpets

14

Luristan Rug

NINETEENTH CENTURY

Size (excluding fringes): 163 x 100mm (6½ x 4in)

Stitch count: 151 x 95

THE NOMADIC Luri tribes in the mountains to the south of Hamadan in western Iran produce rugs with simple, unsophisticated patterns in bold, bright colours. In the original of this design, which was probably woven for private domestic use, there is a curious contrast between the naive field design and the elegant, well-proportioned Greek frieze occupying the border. Together they combine to make a very satisfying and eye-catching design.

■	504	▨	545
■	852	□	842
▨	321	□	988

59

IRAN
Luristan Rug

15

Shiraz Carpet

c. 1900

Size (excluding fringes): 162 x 99mm (6¼ x 4in)

Stitch count: 149 x 95

ALTHOUGH the various nomadic tribes selling their carpets in Shiraz (in the south of Iran) use a number of different patterns, the original of this design displays a field layout often seen in this area, with two linked lozenges extended to arrowheads at each end. The corners of the field may contain animals or birds, as in this case. Shiraz carpets are woven on an all-wool base and the pile is soft, with a lustrous sheen.

■	207	■	643	
■	926	■	955	
■	922	□	989	

61

IRAN
Introduction

Miniature
Oriental Rugs
and Carpets

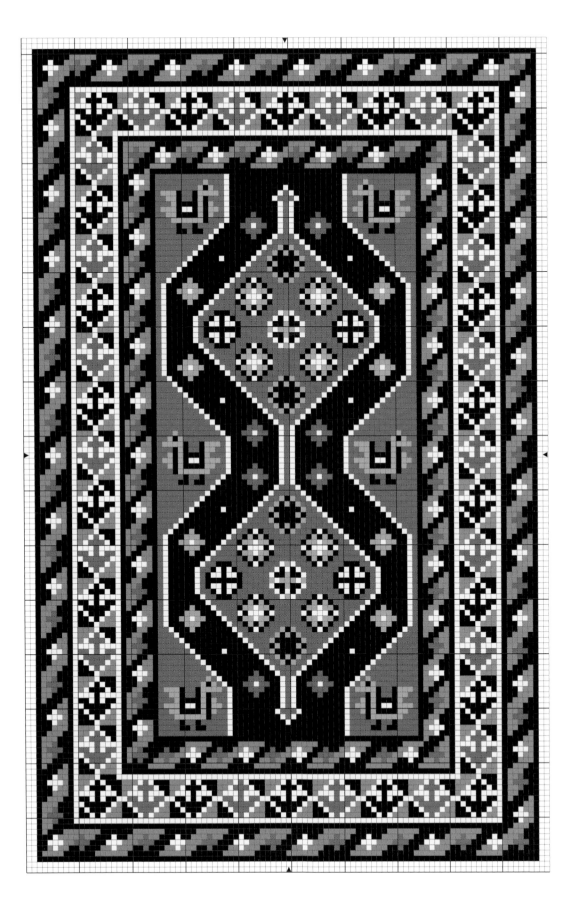

16

Baluchi Carpet

c. 1900

Size (excluding fringes): 181 x 104mm (7 x 4⅛in)

Stitch count: 163 x 99

BALUCHI carpets do not come from Baluchistan; they are woven by tribes in the north-east Iranian province of Khorasan. This example is based on an original displaying strong Turkoman influences, both in the field, which is filled with modified *guls* (see also page 77) and in the border, which is very similar to some Afghan weavings. The colours, however, are typical of Baluchi weaving, as is the outer border which is often described as the 'running dog' pattern.

	305		504
	982		851
	863		

65

IRAN
Baluchi Carpet

17

Baluchi Carpet

MID-TWENTIETH CENTURY

Size (excluding fringes): 144 x 110mm (5¾ x 4¼in)

Stitch count: 137 x 101

THIS DESIGN is based, like the previous one, on a Baluchi carpet woven in Khorasan. It shows a strong Turkoman influence as far as the field is concerned, but uses typical Baluchi colours. The outer border, once again, is in a variation of the 'running dog' pattern.

▬	725	▬	748
▬	916	▭	991
▬	184		

IRAN
Baluchi Carpet

Miniature
Oriental Rugs
and Carpets

18

Baluchi
Prayer Rug

TWENTIETH CENTURY

Size (excluding fringes): 137 x 88mm (5¼ x 3½in)

Stitch count: 126 x 81

MANY BALUCHI carpets are in the form of prayer rugs. They come in a variety of patterns and one of the most frequently found is the 'tree of life', as in this example. The *mihrab*, or niche, in a Baluchi prayer rug is almost always rectangular, unlike the elaborate arch shapes seen in most Anatolian prayer rugs (see page 13).

 504

 824

303

988

851

71

IRAN
Baluchi Prayer
Rug

19

Baluchi 'Boteh' Rug

TWENTIETH CENTURY

Size (excluding fringes): 131 x 83mm (5⅛ x 3¼in)

Stitch count: 119 x 77

THIS DESIGN for a small rug makes attractive use of the Persian *boteh* motif in red and dark brown on a background the colour of camel hair. The border patterns are again typical of Baluchi weaving from the Khorasan area.

■	866	▨	761
■	749	☐	992
■	128		

IRAN
Baluchi 'Boteh'
Rug

Miniature
Oriental Rugs
and Carpets

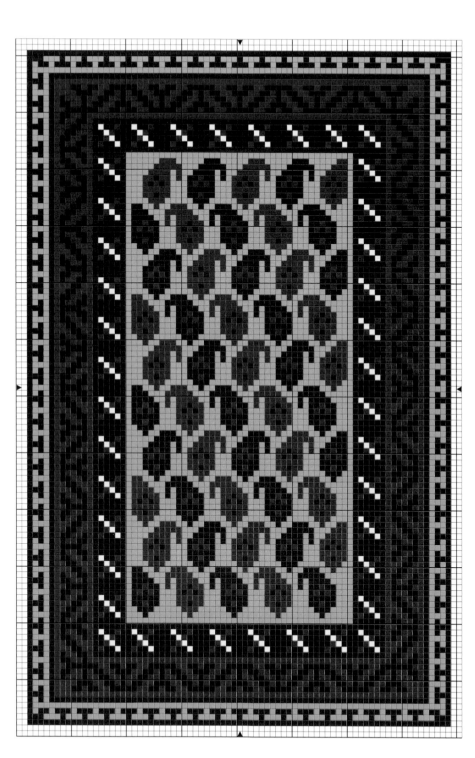

CENTRAL ASIA

Aral Sea

KAZAKHSTAN

KIRGIZSTAN

UZBEKISTAN

YOMUD

TURKMENISTAN

TAJIKISTAN

Kashgar

CHINA
(SINKIANG
PROVINCE)

BESHIR

Khotan

SARYK

Meshed

KHORASAN

Kabul

Herat

AFGHANISTAN

BALUCHI

Lahore

IRAN

PAKISTAN

Introduction

THE REGION of Central Asia (which for the purposes of this book includes Afghanistan and the areas of East and West Turkestan, stretching from the Chinese province of Sinkiang to the eastern shores of the Caspian Sea) was once largely populated by a number of nomadic tribes who relied upon their weaving skills to provide a wide range of items for their own domestic use. These items included bags and containers of many kinds, tent floors and door screens, camel and horse trappings and large pannier bags for use on their migrations. Much of the weaving was functional rather than decorative, but some very fine items were woven for special occasions such as weddings. As the nomadic tribes became settled, they turned to making carpets and rugs for sale, gradually adjusting their sizes and shapes to meet the requirements of the market.

Although each tribe had its own traditional patterns and motifs, the weavings of the whole region show characteristic similarities in style and layout. The background colour is usually a dull red with the field filled with repeated shapes known as *guls*. These may be large or small, simple or complex in design, but are almost always octagons or lozenges. The borders are usually filled with a repeating pattern in black or very dark blue, although some nineteenth-century carpets include brighter colours.

Tribal weaving throughout the region has been badly affected by wars, famines and political upheavals and far fewer genuine carpets are being woven in Afghanistan or Turkestan at the present time. In their place a modern carpet industry has emerged in nearby Pakistan, where many of the traditional Afghan and Turkoman designs are being made under workshop conditions. Six designs from the Central Asian region are included in this collection.

20

Afghan Rug

TWENTIETH CENTURY

Size (excluding fringes): 164 x 99mm (6½ x 4in)

Stitch count: 149 x 95

THIS DESIGN is based on a typical modern rug made in Afghanistan. As with most carpets from Central Asia, Afghans have a dull red field filled with a regular pattern of repeated motifs known as *guls*. The Afghan *guls* are larger than any others and are sometimes described as 'elephants' feet'. They are octagonal and quartered in contrasting colours, with a simple floral pattern. The border patterns are usually in black or a very dark blue.

 759

 748

756

992

CENTRAL
ASIA
Afghan Rug

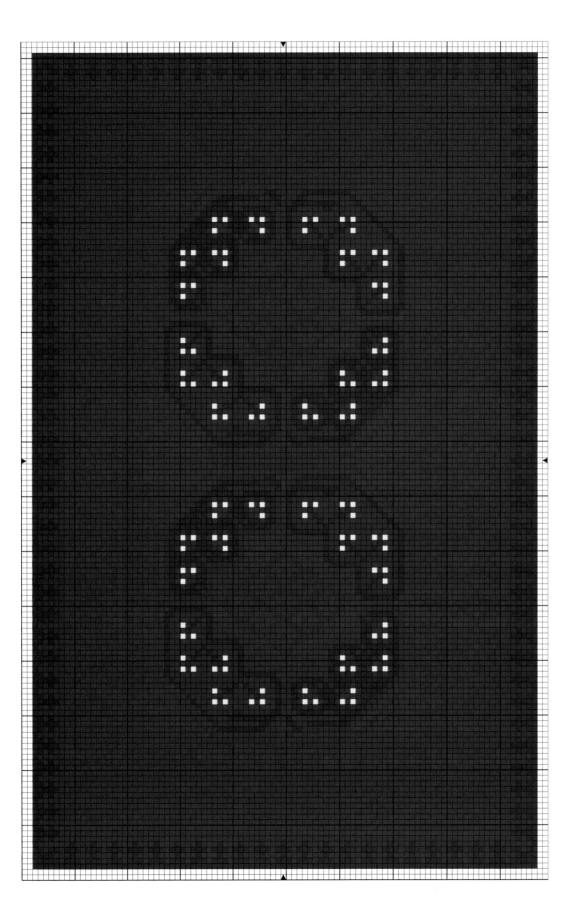

21

Small Afghan Rug

TWENTIETH CENTURY

Size (excluding fringes): 128 x 112mm (5⅛ x 4⅜in)

Stitch count: 121 x 101

WHILE THIS small rug is basically similar to the preceding design, again using the 'elephants' feet' motif, it has been included because it lends itself to enlargement should a bigger carpet be required. The field size can be increased to hold twelve (4 x 3) or even fifteen (5 x 3) *guls*, with only minor adjustments to the border pattern.

■	852	▤	223
■	227	□	991

Miniature
Oriental Rugs
and Carpets

22

Saryk-Turkoman Rug

TWENTIETH CENTURY

Size (excluding fringes): 158 x 103mm (6¼ x 4⅛in)

Stitch count: 145 x 97

THE SARYK are a nomadic Turkoman tribe in the northern border region of Afghanistan. In this two-colour design, the field is filled with unusual 20-sided cruciform *guls* in dark blue on a deep red background. These colours are characteristic of Saryk weavings. The spaces in between the *guls* are occupied by subsidiary motifs to complete a comprehensive field pattern. The borders are similar to those in other Afghan weavings.

| ■ | 725 | ■ | 748 |

85

23

Yomud Rug

TWENTIETH CENTURY

Size (excluding fringes): 163 x 112mm (6½ x 4½in)

Stitch count: 151 x 103

ALTHOUGH most Turkoman weaving is based on a red background, this design with its range of greens and browns is attractively different. The Yomud tribes, who live in Turkmenistan to the east of the Caspian Sea, use a variety of different *guls*, but all are lozenge-shaped and arranged in a diagonal pattern. This design is sometimes described as the 'birds on a pole' pattern.

■ 208		▨ 643	
▨ 763		▨ 641	
■ 916		□ 691	
■ 647			

CENTRAL ASIA
Yomud Rug

Miniature
Oriental Rugs
and Carpets

24

Turkoman Rug

AGE UNKNOWN

Size (excluding fringes): 160 x 114mm (6¼ x 4½in)

Stitch count: 148 x 108

THIS DESIGN, with its simplified cruciform, lozenge-shaped *guls*, has been derived from a carpet believed to have been acquired in Kashgar, the most westerly city in China, close to the border with Kirgizstan. It displays some similarity to Yomud or Beshir weavings, but its exact origin and age are obscure.

When working this rug be careful to note that the field has an even number of stitches in each direction (normally the field has an odd number of stitches to allow for the centre lines).

 505

 748

504

988

91

CENTRAL ASIA
Turkoman Rug

25

Khotan Carpet

TWENTIETH CENTURY

Size (excluding fringes): 193 x 104mm (7½ x 4⅛in)

Stitch count: 175 x 97

THE CARPETS of East Turkestan, now part of the Chinese province of Sinkiang, show some Chinese influence in their decoration, including the use of muted colours, as in this example. The details of the design, however, show a clear relationship with both the Caucasus and Anatolia in the geometric stars and the decorative Kufic border (see also page 3).

	992		903
	187		693
	766		921

Miniature
Oriental Rugs
and Carpets

Equivalent Shade Numbers

For Appletons crewel wool and DMC and Anchor
stranded cottons

APPLETONS	DMC	ANCHOR
Reds and pinks		
149	902	897
203	758	9575
207	356	5975
208	919	341
209	355	5968
223	223	895
227	221	896
503	817	47
504	321	19
505	815	44
725	355	341
755	3688	68
756	3687	69
759	3685	70
863	356	5975
866	347	13
Browns		
128	918	341
184	841	378

185	840	379
186	839	380
187	838	381
303	975	355
305	801	359
761	422	373
763	436	369
766	434	370
903	420	375
914	420	375
916	869	944
935	902	897
955	610	905
982	642	392

White/ecru

988	762	234
989	762	234
991	BlancNeige	2
992	Ecru or 712	387 or 926

Yellows

311	729	890
473	7725	8042
691	3047	886
692	7493	8038
693	3046	887
696	680	901
842	677	300
843	676	891
851	739	366

Equivalent
Shade Numbers

Greens

295	936	268
332	834	874
334	831	808
358	935	269
404	469	267
544	471	265
545	470	266
546	469	267
547	937	268
641	503	876
643	502	877
644	501	878
647	500	879

Blues

321	932	268
462	794	176
742	794	176
747	336	150
748	336	150
749	823	127
824	797	132
852	823	127
921	318	235
922	932	920
923	931	921
925	312	1036
926	311	1035
928	823	127

About the Authors

Meik and Ian McNaughton, now retired, have lived in the Hampshire village of Chawton since 1963. Ian met Meik, who was born and grew up in Holland, while he was serving with the Royal Engineers in that country in the summer of 1945. They were married in the following year. Army life took them and their two daughters to Cyprus from 1955 to 1958 and to Germany from 1960 to 1963, when Ian retired from the army as a lieutenant-colonel to join the Railway Inspectorate of the Ministry of Transport. He finally retired from the position of Chief Inspecting Officer of Railways in 1982.

Ian has had a lifelong interest in oriental carpets. Meik has been sewing since her school days, when she learnt dressmaking and smocking. She starting doing tapestry in the late 1950s and then took up counted cross stitch and patchwork in the late 1970s. Miniature oriental carpets appeared on the scene more recently, when a granddaughter reached 'dolls' house' age.

Index

101

Index

Acknowledgements

Thanks are due to the Trustees of the National Gallery, London, for permission to reproduce *The Annunciation, with Saint Emidius* by Carlo Crivelli as the frontispiece to this book.

Some of our miniaturized designs are based on photographs of full-size carpets which we found in various reference books. While every effort has been made to contact the copyright holders of these pictures, in some cases this has not been possible due to the length of time since the publication of the books in question. We will be happy to include any further acknowledgement details in a reprint if necessary. The following list comprises a complete record of sources used.

Digby, G.W., *French Tapestries from the Fourteenth to Eighteenth Centuries*, London, Batsford, 1951, plate 12 (see design 2, page 17)

Formenton, F., *Oriental Rugs and Carpets*, London, Hamlyn, 1972, page 219 (see design 17, page 67)

Gans-Ruedin, E., *Oriental Carpets*, Orbis Pictus Series No.14, Berne, Hallwag, 1965, plate VII (see design 11, page 46)

Gregorian, A.T., *Oriental Rugs and the Stories They Tell*, London, Frederick Warne, 1978, pages 181 (see design 7, page 34), 168 (see design 8, page 37), and 41 (see design 14, page 58)

Herbert, J. S., *Oriental Rugs: The Illustrated Guide*, New York, Macmillan, 1978, plates 66 (see design 16, page 64), 64 (see design 19, page 73) and 88 (see design 25, page 93)

Kybalova, L. and Darbois, D., *Carpets of the Orient*, London, Hamlyn, 1969, plate 42 (see design 23, page 87)

Liebetrau, P., *Oriental Rugs in Colour*, London, Collier-Macmillan, 1963, plates 48 (see design 9, page 40), 44 (see design 18, page 70) and 40 (see design 20, page 78)

Milhofer, S. A., *The Colour Treasury of Oriental Rugs*, Oxford, Elsevier-Phaidon, 1976, page 110 (see design 22, page 84)

Schürmann, U., *Oriental Carpets*, London, Octopus, 1979, pages 63 (see design 3, page 20), 169 (see design 5, page 28) and 161 (see design 10, page 43)

Thompson, J., *Carpets from the Tents, Cottages and Workshops of Asia*, London, Laurence King, 1993, page 22 (see design 6, page 31)

BOOKS

WOODWORKING

40 More Woodworking Plans & Projects	*GMC Publications*	Making Chairs and Tables	*GMC Publications*
Bird Boxes and Feeders for the Garden	*Dave Mackenzie*	Making Fine Furniture	*Tom Darby*
Complete Woodfinishing	*Ian Hosker*	Making Little Boxes from Wood	*John Bennett*
Electric Woodwork	*Jeremy Broun*	Making Shaker Furniture	*Barry Jackson*
Furniture Projects	*Rod Wales*	Pine Furniture Projects for the Home	*Dave Mackenzie*
Furniture Restoration (Practical Crafts)	*Kevin Jan Bonner*	Sharpening Pocket Reference Book	*Jim Kingshott*
Furniture Restoration and Repair for Beginners	*Kevin Jan Bonner*	Sharpening: The Complete Guide	*Jim Kingshott*
Green Woodwork	*Mike Abbott*	Woodfinishing Handbook (Practical Crafts)	*Ian Hosker*
The Incredible Router	*Jeremy Broun*	Woodworking Plans and Projects	*GMC Publications*
Making & Modifying Woodworking Tools	*Jim Kingshott*	The Workshop	*Jim Kingshott*

WOODTURNING

Adventures in Woodturning	*David Springett*	Practical Tips for Turners & Carvers	*GMC Publications*
Bert Marsh: Woodturner	*Bert Marsh*	Practical Tips for Woodturners	*GMC Publications*
Bill Jones' Notes from the Turning Shop	*Bill Jones*	Spindle Turning	*GMC Publications*
Bill Jones' Further Notes from the Turning Shop	*Bill Jones*	Turning Miniatures in Wood	*John Sainsbury*
Colouring Techniques for Woodturners	*Jan Sanders*	Turning Wooden Toys	*Terry Lawrence*
Decorative Techniques for Woodturners	*Hilary Bowen*	Understanding Woodturning	*Ann & Bob Phillips*
Essential Tips for Woodturners	*GMC Publications*	Useful Techniques for Woodturners	*GMC Publications*
Faceplate Turning	*GMC Publications*	Useful Woodturning Projects	*GMC Publications*
Fun at the Lathe	*R. C. Bell*	Woodturning Jewellery	*Hilary Bowen*
Illustrated Woodturning Techniques	*John Hunnex*	Woodturning Masterclass	*Tony Boase*
Intermediate Woodturning Projects	*GMC Publications*	Woodturning Techniques	*GMC Publications*
Keith Rowley's Woodturning Projects	*Keith Rowley*	Woodturning Test Reports	*GMC Publications*
Make Money from Woodturning	*Ann & Bob Phillips*	Woodturning Wizardry	*David Springett*
Multi-Centre Woodturning	*Ray Hopper*	Woodturning: A Foundation Course	*Keith Rowley*
Pleasure and Profit from Woodturning	*Reg Sherwin*	Woodturning: A Source Book of Shapes	*John Hunnex*

WOODCARVING

The Art of the Woodcarver	*GMC Publications*	Useful Techniques for Woodcarvers	*GMC Publications*
Carving Birds & Beasts	*GMC Publications*	Wildfowl Carving - Volume 1	*Jim Pearce*
Carving on Turning	*Chris Pye*	Wildfowl Carving - Volume 2	*Jim Pearce*
Carving Realistic Birds	*David Tippey*	The Woodcarvers	*GMC Publications*
Decorative Woodcarving	*Jeremy Williams*	Woodcarving for Beginners	*GMC Publications*
Essential Tips for Woodcarvers	*GMC Publications*	Woodcarving Test Reports	*GMC Publications*
Essential Woodcarving Techniques	*Dick Onians*	Woodcarving Tools, Materials & Equipment	*Chris Pye*
Lettercarving in Wood: A Practical Course	*Chris Pye*	Woodcarving: A Complete Course	*Ron Butterfield*
Practical Tips for Turners & Carvers	*GMC Publications*	Woodcarving: A Foundation Course	*Zoë Gertner*
Understanding Woodcarving	*GMC Publications*		

UPHOLSTERY

Seat Weaving (Practical Crafts)	*Ricky Holdstock*	Upholstery Techniques & Projects	*David James*
Upholsterer's Pocket Reference Book	*David James*	Upholstery: A Complete Course	*David James*
Upholstery Restoration	*David James*		

TOYMAKING

Designing & Making Wooden Toys	*Terry Kelly*
Fun to Make Wooden Toys & Games	*Jeff & Jennie Loader*
Making Board, Peg & Dice Games	*Jeff & Jennie Loader*
Making Character Bears	*Valerie Tyler*
Making Wooden Toys & Games	*Jeff & Jennie Loader*
Restoring Rocking Horses	*Clive Green & Anthony Dew*

DOLLS' HOUSES

Architecture for Dolls' Houses	*Joyce Percival*
Beginners' Guide to the Dolls' House Hobby	*Jean Nisbett*
The Complete Dolls' House Book	*Jean Nisbett*
Dolls' House Bathrooms: Lots of Little Loos	*Patricia King*
Easy to Make Dolls' House Accessories	*Andrea Barham*
Make Your Own Dolls' House Furniture	*Maurice Harper*
Making Dolls' House Furniture	*Patricia King*
Making Georgian Dolls' Houses	*Derek Rowbottom*
Making Miniature Oriental Rugs & Carpets	*Meik & Ian McNaughton*
Making Period Dolls' House Accessories	*Andrea Barham*
Making Period Dolls' House Furniture	*Derek & Sheila Rowbottom*
Making Tudor Dolls' Houses	*Derek Rowbottom*
Making Unusual Miniatures	*Graham Spalding*
Making Victorian Dolls' House Furniture	*Patricia King*
Miniature Needlepoint Carpets	*Janet Granger*
The Secrets of the Dolls' House Makers	*Jean Nisbett*

CRAFTS

Celtic Knotwork Designs	*Sheila Sturrock*
Collage from Seeds, Leaves and Flowers	*Joan Carver*
Complete Pyrography	*Stephen Poole*
Creating Knitwear Designs	*Pat Ashforth & Steve Plummer*
Cross Stitch Kitchen Projects	*Janet Granger*
Cross Stitch on Colour	*Sheena Rogers*
Embroidery Tips & Hints	*Harold Hayes*
Making Greetings Cards for Beginners	*Pat Sutherland*
Making Knitwear Fit	*Pat Ashforth & Steve Plummer*
Pyrography Handbook (Practical Crafts)	*Stephen Poole*
Tassel Making for Beginners	*Enid Taylor*
Tatting Collage	*Lindsay Rogers*

THE HOME

Home Ownership: Buying and Maintaining	*Nicholas Snelling*
Security for the Householder: Fitting Locks and Other Devices	*E. Phillips*

VIDEOS

Drop-in and Pinstuffed Seats	*David James*
Stuffover Upholstery	*David James*
Elliptical Turning	*David Springett*
Woodturning Wizardry	*David Springett*
Turning Between Centres: The Basics	*Dennis White*
Turning Bowls	*Dennis White*
Boxes, Goblets and Screw Threads	*Dennis White*
Novelties and Projects	*Dennis White*
Classic Profiles	*Dennis White*
Twists and Advanced Turning	*Dennis White*
Sharpening the Professional Way	*Jim Kingshott*
Sharpening Turning & Carving Tools	*Jim Kingshott*
Bowl Turning	*John Jordan*
Hollow Turning	*John Jordan*
Woodturning: A Foundation Course	*Keith Rowley*
Carving a Figure: The Female Form	*Ray Gonzalez*
The Router: A Beginner's Guide	*Alan Goodsell*
The Scroll Saw: A Beginner's Guide	*John Burke*

MAGAZINES

WOODTURNING ◆ WOODCARVING ◆ TOYMAKING
FURNITURE & CABINETMAKING ◆ BUSINESSMATTERS
CREATIVE IDEAS FOR THE HOME ◆ THE ROUTER

The above represents a full list of all titles currently published or scheduled to be published. All are available direct from the Publishers or through bookshops, newsagents and specialist retailers. To place an order, or to obtain a complete catalogue, contact:

GMC Publications,
166 High Street, Lewes, East Sussex BN7 1XU United Kingdom
Tel: 01273 488005 Fax: 01273 478606

Orders by credit card are accepted